Snake in the Spine, Wolf in the Heart

political poems

Barry Goldensohn

artwork

Douglas Kinsey

Fomite

Poems copyright 2016 © by Barry Goldensohn
Art copyright 2016 © by Douglas Kinsey

All rights reserved. No part of this book may be reproduced in any form or by any means without the prior written consent of the publisher, except in the case of brief quotations used in reviews and certain other noncommercial uses permitted by copyright law.

ISBN-13: 978-1-942515-56-2
Library of Congress Control Number: 2016944430

Fomite
58 Peru Street
Burlington, VT 05401
www.fomitepress.com

Cover Art - Douglas Kinsey

*To my children, Matthew and Rachel,
their children Tiana and Ava, Ty and Tracy, and their children,
Nadeya, Dylan, Ethan, Jordan, Raheem, and Teagan.
They are the anchor of my hope for a magnanimous and
compassionate future.*

Books by Barry Goldensohn

Saint Venus Eve
Uncarving the Block
The Marrano
Dance Music (a chapbook)
East Long Pond, with Lorrie Goldensohn (a chapbook)
The Listener Aspires to the Condition of Music
The Hundred Yard Dash Man

ACKNOWLEDGEMENTS

NYRB: Driving Westward to San Diego

Salmagundi: Tarzan & Co., Ignorance, Margaret Roper, After the Revolution, The Entitled, The Marrano, Ancient City, sections of Meditations on Violence

Slate.com: Old Home Day. Reading Faust when Young

Agenda (London): Pieces for the Suicide of Paul Celan

Poetry: Arch of Titus, War and Peace

Ploughshares: U.S. Signal Corps Footage

The Hardy Review: At the Frick

Notre Dame Review: The Statue

Suss: A Treatise on Ungovernment

AGNI: Fugitive Night Song

Contents

Preface	1
Artist Statement	2
Tarzan & Co.	5
Driving Westward To San Diego	7
Old Home Day	9
David And Saul	10
The Summer I Spent Screwing In The Back Seats Of Station Wagons	11
Wedding	13
Pieces For The Suicide Of Paul Celan	15
Fugitive's Night Song	18
A Treatise On Ungovernment	20
Forbidden Games	24
The Statue	26
Memorial	27
Marriage Vows, 1956	28
Arch Of Titus	30
War and Peace	31
Letter To My Sister	34
East Village, NYC, 1962	36
U.S. Signal Corps Footage	37
A Vision	38
The Child	40
Ignorance	41
His Balance	42
Mourning Song	43
At The Frick	45
Margaret Roper	46
The Killers	48
The Body Politic	49
The Simple Life In Strongsville, Ohio	50

Reading Faust When Young	51
After The Revolution	53
Child Soldiers	54
War Work	55
The Information Age	56
Diplomacy	58
April 26, 2006	59
The Entitled	60
Heritage	61
The Marrano	64
From The Book Of Blessings	66
The Execution of Lady Jane Grey	67
Ancient City	69
Scandal	70
Gesualdo In Concert	71
Burmese Temple Bell	72
Meditations On Violence	77
About the Author	98
About the Artist	99

Preface

This is a book of political poems. It deals with distortions of consciousness and feeling in response to our past hundred years and more of war, our history and its nightmares, confusion and occasional visions of peace, inner and outer. Do not expect to find anything like Milton's mighty trumpet, commanding God to avenge the massacre of the Anabaptists by massacring Catholics: *Avenge, O Lord, thy slaughtered saints, etc.* God is no longer required for these tasks done in his name. Absent here as well is anything like Swift's savage indignation at Marlborough as in *A Satirical Elegy on the Death of a Late Famous General* which is more understandable than Milton's use of politics in poems but of little use to me over the decades in which these poems were written. The governing spirits in these poems are horror, confusion, absurdity and nightmare.

Artist Statement

The content of the poetry and that of the monotype images have much in common even though the images and narratives are disparate. The monotypes are not intended to be illustrations of the poems. The images are derived from years of sketchbooks, but many of them also depend on photographs found in places such as in the New York Times. Naturally the photographs suggest narratives of specific places, but I deliberately removed all written material while collecting them. In some cases I can't even remember the conflict they emerged from or what culture they represent. I hoped for ambiguity and universal experience. Obviously, there can be no specific interpretation of a work of art like a monotype. Every observer gives it some uniqueness through his or her own experience and imagnation. Subject matter is not synonymous with meaning.

Tarzan & Co.

I lived in the caress
of the most dangerous
wolves, apes, big cats,
knowing them in my hands,
the thick ruff at the throat,
the soft skin of the belly,
the vulnerable crotch
taking on their powers
with their fearsome tenderness
like the English nobleman
with rich Edwardian speech,
who turned toward savageness
against the systematic
savage trade from home.
This was after the war
after the famous photos
of death camps and the entrance
of the new word "genocide"—
our apartment overcrowded
with Jewish refugees
sleeping on the floor.
Growing away from childhood
I turned for my defense
to a sterner animal code,
more instinctive, perilous,
than the mild rational world
of my accommodating home.
Sometimes I would stand
at the corner for an hour
buried in my book

until some thoughtful neighbor
would grab me by the elbow
to steer me across the street
still absent in the dream
of an animal poise of the body,
faster, more alert,
enough to seize the cobra
arched and ready to strike,
to save the young, swimming,
with a knife across the belly
of the treacherous crocodile,
and knowing a hidden language
that I had been denied,
the message of the spoor,
the turn of twig and vine.
This was the dream of knowledge
I returned from as a beast
 to change the world to beasts.

Driving Westward To San Diego

Plutonic rubble, boulders, gravel,
dust storms, sandstorms, stone and bone dry
desolation, post-nuclear waste, post-fire-storm,
the tors and pillars of a city we erased
with fire from the air. Human work.
But we are blameless for this dead debris.
The earth's heart, under its thin skin,
with magma red intensity,
overheats its igneous rock
beyond the limits of our own ferocity.
Driving westward on the interstate
above the east escarpment of the Coastal Range
we cross the ridge into a lush valley
green with Pacific rains,
land that seems like God's work,
in whose name we killed for it and cleared it:
lining streets with oleander, almond,
rows of ginkgo, fig, euphorbia,
white moons of giant clematis,
domesticated flames of rose and lily beds,
undulating fence lines, squared-off farms,
nothing here but what we ourselves devised,
all dimensions ample and humane.

Old Home Day

They gather around the Common, and the young
lay down their frisbees for the cloud parade
of life as it's always been with nothing to change—
volunteer firemen and ambulance brigade,
the town cop, vets of foreign wars,
some recent ones that snared the world
with bombs, drones, mortars, BARs.
The wars against their own lead the parade,
vets of the Revolution and Civil War, Texas
against Cheyenne, King Philip's War,
with their flintlocks, muskets, sabers, arrows, bows,
and the band played and the beer flowed like blood,
in this sweet town where everyone knows
everyone's public name and secret name
and all their dead and no one locks their doors.
No one stands aside to see. All join
this participatory democracy.
Two brothers dead in one campaign
mosey over, AWOL as usual, for beer
and to read their names on the brass plaque again
fixed to an obelisk in the square.

David And Saul

When David sings Saul grasps his spear—
Observed discreetly by members of the Court
The pundits blame Saul's madness,
but others, outside the court, say it's power—
the god-talk and the liberating tunes
enrage Saul as David sings.
His flagrant dazzle, rapture and spells
trivialize the authority of kings.
Saul gnashes his teeth, knots his face.
Think of poor Stalin, unable to kill
lucky Shostakovich. If not for the music,
if it were just poems, he could kill.

The Summer I Spent Screwing In The Back Seats Of Station Wagons

was the last summer that lasted all summer.
This was not--do not misread the title--
screwing the seats in, but climbing in
the back seats and screwing as fast as I could.
It was always the same, open the back and fling
in the power driver and the big tool
box with the braces and screws as the tall Pole
pressed the window firmly into place
as I would drill the holes, line up the clamps,
and screw them in. If the clamps sat too tight
the window cracked and then a flurry of work
as we swarmed ahead of our spot on the line
the tall Pole and I at Fisher Bodies
in Euclid, Ohio, and rushed to return to our place.
I kept bashing my hands and my nights were crushed,
and in all that soul exhausting work
the cars were as rotten as we could make them.
There was nothing of ourselves we wanted to see
in what we did to Chevy Kingswood and Nomad
and Pontiac Safari with pubescent tailfins.
This was in Euclid, who looked on Beauty bare,
Ohio, whose three long syllables danced
in only four letters, pronounced Ah-hah,
by my fellow workers who wrenched, torqued, and screwed
on the assembly line with me in Euclid, Ohio.
At the end of the day all we had was numbers,
corporate totals. It brought to mind
the boast of Wilt the Stilt that he had fucked
twenty thousand women in his time,

and never, never, the same woman twice.
And as we looked, wearied, at our line of cars
we wondered, how could he tell?

Wedding

Hallowed by the marriage clerk at City Hall
they stand at the top of the broad marble stairs
for snapshots by their friends.
No parents around. They come from elsewhere
and by alien custom dress like church folk
for this civil fix. She holds his palm to her breasts
with one hand, the other rests low on her belly
which, under the sumptuous red dress
appears from her gesture to hold a child.
He looks at her, enfolding, mild.
They could be Rebecca and Isaac
founding a tribe in a strange land
or Hector and Andromache, thick
with their people, blind to the brute hand.

Pieces For The Suicide Of Paul Celan

> When Celan asked Heidegger, who was Rector of the University of Freiberg in the early Hitler years, about his postwar silence concerning his Nazi past, Heidegger either refused to answer or was evasive. George Steiner says, "Either way, the effect on Celan can be felt to have been calamitous."

Roundness of eyes between bars
greets
the snake in the spine
the wolf in the heart

That mind so naked
and the room dark

you are allowed to touch it

that appearance of nakedness
under an impenetrable code

He cannot speak to you
not even tell you this
it would tell too much
and all of it wrong

distorted phrasing,
the hesitations badly
out of place

Illegible, this
world, it all doubles

Did he ask the Rector:
Why did you assist
the cursed marriage
of the mutable state
to the immutable spirit—driving
the one mad as the other dies
driving them both mad
blind and violent

The Rector was
so committed to unity
of the whole, the body
was the state, the lovely
discordant University
allowed one voice only,
under the single will of the state

the whole as meaningless
to itself as a tree

to overcome the insult
of diversity

       (Look at them sullen
       on their bunks, some
       facing left, some right,
       or staring at your eyes, your throat)

and answered the aphorist
of image with silence

locked in his own depths
and climbing out
forever

August:

Is that a bird?
No, it is the brightest of the leaves
falling early

The last interrogation was unclear
the translator belonged to the court
no one understood
what the prisoner said--
he was carrion in a dog's mouth,
eaten, puked up and eaten again

Why are you waiting? Sew,
sew it on, he's torn
away his face, if you wait
too long the face will rot
the stitches won't hold
you know why he tore it
and why he wants it back

Fugitive's Night Song

No blood spilt,
no patrols.
A mattress and quilt
on the dark blue tiles
in the crowded room
when you arrive,
your family all alive,
you home.

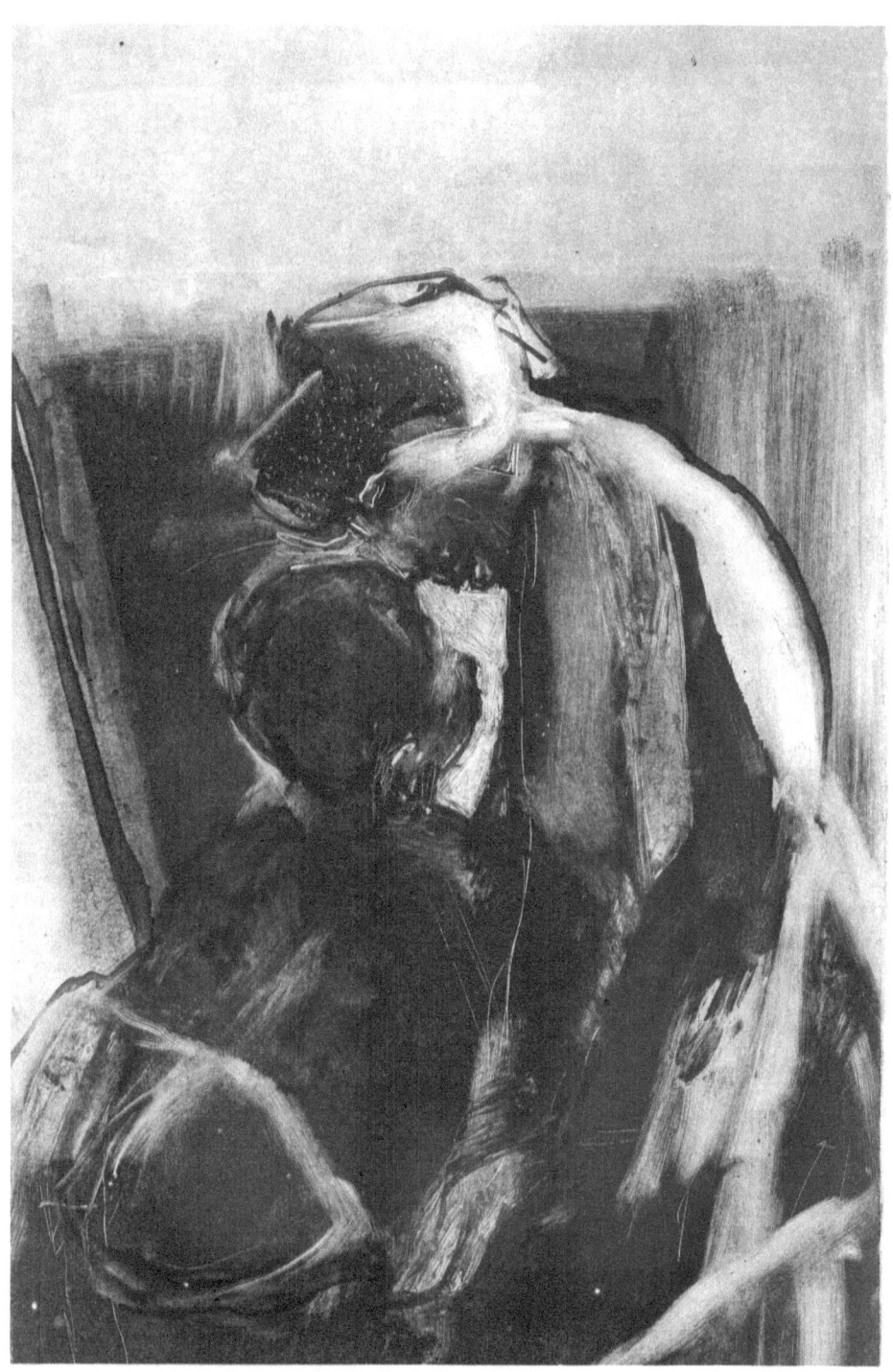

A Treatise On Ungovernment
Que scais-je? Montaigne

A white haired man in a rich cloth coat
paces gravely on the platform waiting
for the No.1 train, his hands
splay open with quiet eloquence
and he speaks to one unseen by us
with the sound of a breeze through leaves.

What can not be understood can not be governed. Plato

A young couple, faces nearly touching,
speak to one another in Bengali
and Bengali flavored English, giving the words
a new music, with faces lifted
from Indian paintings
into American clothes, on a New York
street corner, waiting for the light to change.

What good are roots if you can't take them with you. Gertrude Stein
...a nation is the same people living in the same place. L. Boom

As the train lurches through its dark curves
a young woman grasping the pole
swings towards me in my seat
and her large breasts sway in a lacy
loose knit white blouse and nearly brush my face
offering an intangible perfume.

"Rabbi, Rabbi," she cried.
"Do not touch me." John, xx,16-17

He knows the city in intimate bits:
store windows, empty streets, a man
seated on a step in front of a store,
a woman in a window overlooking rooftops,
a couple settling in their red, plush seats
in formal clothes, before the theater crowd
presses in. An usherette against the wall.

Canonically conjugate variables are pairs of properties,
like position and momentum, energy and time, linked in such a way
that they can not both be measured at the same time. W. Heisenberg

Accident. The torn boy dies, shattered, under
pressure bandages, pouring IV's, morphine,
the paramedic knows if he were someone else,
a surgeon, somewhere else, the OR,
the boy mangled in the road would live.

Omniscience is a fantasy of total power. Max
The city is ungovernable. J.V. Lindsay

Shaving the outer skin of his fingertips
with a plastic lady's razor a thin man
with a gray stubble beard and hair—
is he a safe cracker preparing to feel within
the lock a delicate shift, or a lover
getting to the most sensitive layer
for the most intimate caress? What
would he not discover with those fingers—
what rods, tumblers, oiled wards.

Knowledge is Power. Bacon
With much knowledge there is much suffering. Rublev

"To confirm the conspiracy they wanted,"
he said over his moonshine martini,
"the intelligence was crap and we
couldn't move on it but we needed
to plant stories around the world so we confirmed
what we knew was crap, and all the newsmen
swallowed corrupt intelligence and the war."

On s'engage puis on voit. Napoleon

Because he revered their music, its plunge through his heart,
legs, throat in endless reverberation,
and their temples that flaunt in stone women entwined
with men, homage to flesh, and their philosophical mind,
cathedrals in which the stone flies upward like fire,
he was sure the population would not endure
the government roundups, pre-dawn arrests,
barely clandestine slaughter of whispering opponents
and the ruling thugs merely a brief transition
out of confusion to a new suitable order
reflecting the soul of the people, his own soul,
so he endured for years in disciplined silence
and inner exile and when he refused to raise
his voice in total assent, his total silence.

All wars are boyish and are fought by boys Melville

Stumpy silhouettes against bright windows
of a megastore way down the street—no light
between three figures, young boys in a clump

arms flailing and punching and one breaks
away and charges back full force
into the cluster of boy with windmilling arms
and another tumbles back then plunges in.
I'm too far away to see if it's a game
or fight or a game of fighting, proving themselves
against the bodies of others, two boys
against one or all against all.

The future is what happens behind our backs. The past is what we face.
Verso Marinetti

Forbidden Games: at the Berlin Holocaust Memorial
an dieses atemlose blinde Spiel...Rilke

It is permitted to move through the field of steles,
the Monument, on foot only at a decorous pace.
The younger children dart among the flat,
dark grey cement boxes, the steles,
climb the lower ones and leap
from each to each, set at the perfect distance.
Among the taller steles deeper in the field
where the path rises and falls with the footing uncertain
and the light narrows to a thin line above
children play peek-a-boo and older kids
snap digital photos poking a head out
or a bare leg with giggles and selfies
to preserve themselves forever
and now and then a child will disappear.

The guards shoo off an older girl who stands
on a stele, another lying down. Both forbidden.
A lost child reappears on the far side
at the corner of Hannah-Arendt-Strasse
and Berliner Strasse and returns shouting
"I'm here, I'm here, over here," unpuzzling
his friends. *Do not make loud noises,*
or shout or yell. No portable radios. No
lying or standing on the steles. No
jumping from one to another. No sunning
in bathing suits. No skateboards.
Do not dirty, soil or pollute. Commands
of the Security Service must be obeyed.
And parents with their children refuse to vanish.

The Statue

Poor Berthold Brecht is now bronze
and sits on a bronze bench now black
outside the Berliner Ensemble. Twice
life-size, his knees where children have climbed,
gleam, also where they have stepped, his toes.
There's room to his left on the bench where others sat
that also gleams. In these new times,
the Berlin Wall down, his State kaput,
he would not like to sit near those to his left,
gleaming. His stare is inward and he smiles
like a smug Buddha who has forgiven
the disaster of his consent.

He is dishonored. His great poems were not
written by this bronze giant. Inscribed
around his seat is his poem "Questions of the Worker-
Reader." The rhetorical questions
insult the worker's intelligence—
a party line poem, and the party's over.
Every morning he is buried in heavy mist
that rises from the river Spree.

MEMORIAL
>   They are the dead you cry to.
>   *The Trojan Women*, Euripides

The bronze spear through armor, sword
slashing through the neck, roadside
explosives of increasing ingenuity, in the market
intelligent human bombs, collapsing
lungs in cities in flame, or heat
and blast so great that bones burn
and nothing is left of the body to mourn.

Outside, carpenters dismantle a scaffold,
a cooper seals flashing and gutters, a mason
tuck-points the uprights, smoothing.
Inside, all leaps skyward,
tall gothic arches rising
from thin pillars, spandrels of air,
a wall of air to carry the delicate vaulted roof.

As we walk around bantering
with craftsmen we wonder how
a town with only farms and a small mill
and summer people crowded around a lake
produced such solemn beauty,
a cage where the wind sings, a vault of air
to bury all that vanishes.

Marriage Vows, 1956

We were claimed by our time, elected
study over prayer, not invulnerable
to the charm of the sacred, of ritual,
even of ceremony when talk of god
was left out. We were married
by a rabbi I revered, who took our youth
and levity as serious, rightly.
After we spoke our dignified vows
and I smashed a glass under my foot
the rabbi yoked us by the powers
granted to him by the Laws of Moses,
of Israel and of the State of New York:
of Moses (in Leviticus), of Israel
(meaning the mystical body of the Jewish people,
not the divided, embattled nation of the Middle East
that clamored for our faith with the Freud
-and-Marx dream of the kibbutz) and the State
of New York (meaning where we were born,
whose rich Diaspora culture we loved—
little theaters, coffee shops, and talk, talk, talk—
and where we lived with unforced loyalty.)

Arch Of Titus

Disregarding the curse
that god will remove your name
from the list of the Chosen People
for passing through the arch,
families of tourists,
People Not Chosen,
pass through blithely
as blithely conquering Romans
in the all-encircling frieze
destroy the Second Temple
and carry away their prize,
menorah and chained slaves
as beautiful as themselves.

Though I've no god to lose
nor community of Jews
and never shared the need
for community of faith
I can not stray through
in my usual careless way
and deny what I have lost.

WAR AND PEACE (from the memoirs of a Jewish officer
                in the Czar's army)

I was a scout and messenger. A shell
burst and I lost my horse, my gun, and woke
sunk in thick alders that bent under me
like a soft couch--unhurt, but nearly choked
by the strap of the leather pouch around my throat.
I crawled into the dusk, losing all
my boyhood faster than I could grasp
in the silence and stinging fog
of the bombed woods. Half the oaks
with their first small spring leaves
burst and burned. It smelled like a dead city,
smoky and abandoned. I found
the path that led to a spot on the river
too swift to cross on foot. Our cavalry
appeared with an old lieutenant who had turned
their rout into an orderly retreat.

He hung back, dismounted, and we talked
about the tasks we were assigned,
while high on their horses the troop filed across.
Nearing dark, a mist rose from the river.
His face, immobile, shone in the cold
like oiled jade--slabs of soft stone
you could mark with your fingernail;
flat cheeks, a broad nose and high forehead.
I was one of the chosen people--could not fail
my mission and thought of this only, he
of something else that I have struggled since then
to grasp. Was he one of the *lamed vov,*

the holy ones disguised, even from themselves,
scattered through the world who save us with wonders?

His horse had wandered off. He whistled
and it charged up from the river, dumb and eager.
A Golem. Could he have called up two that way?
He gave me the horse and I protested faintly.
Then he ordered me. I stopped my protest.
I was young and full of urgency
with front line messages that bore
on the success of war. He was firm,
that was all, and he leaned back on a hummock
of tall grass as I mounted and plunged through
the river, came up dry on the other side,
and galloped after the troops but kept him with me
as I reenact that ending, carrying both,
two horses, or two on one horse,
or me, or him, flying above the river
with a breast stroke through the air.

I accepted this order without question
as something due in the proper conduct of war
and great affairs. Now he buries himself
inside me, the city of the dead endowing
the city of the living with its gods.

Letter To My Sister

In our Father's schoolteacher hand,
on the margins of disinterred snapshots,
nineteen forty-three and forty-four,
the World War murderous still, incinerating
people in cities, remote, unknown,
opposed to us ("And when you've killed
enough they stop fighting" said LeMay),

yet here with Aunt Gert and Uncle Irv
in Williamsport, PA, American peace
in the family embrace, staring children
propped in front of bleak trees
Thanksgiving, Easter break and one July,
an apple tree in leaf and in it me
in the branches grinning, dreaming I was a cat.

You were two and three, my toy still,
to tickle till you fought for breath,
a miniature person, your dresses like an adult's,
fine embroidered blouse and polished shoes.
At seven I wore a tie swung off center.

In one family portrait a leafless road.
Father looked stern, his arms enclosed
Mother before her nose job and sweet Gert,
in front Renee, a child jewel, me smiling,
dully, and you too young for Uncle Irv
to keep in order, staring off, straining
to swallow your fist. And floating on point
above these family groupings, Mother as Giselle

in a long chiffon dress with a ruffled hem.

This was the Home Front. I collected papers
in a red flyer wagon from the neighbors
for our soldier uncles and the War Effort.
During the war I was chased down, even here,
by four older boys yelling "He killed Jesus."
They threw stones but all missed. One boy,
when they caught me, prevented real mischief
by insisting that "Jesus was a Jew."
His passionate logic prevailed.

These loving sisters and their husbands
all died in their beds surrounded by love,
and because the tribal terrors bred in that old world
were blurred and weakened in this heartland,
no one here imagined the powers abroad:
gas chambers, fire storms, the committed merciless soul.

EAST VILLAGE, NYC, 1962

Facing the clotted street, an abundant blonde
and a lean black man, every summer afternoon
with great bravura at their open window
make love for their neighbors, the soldiers
in the army of the arts who watch in silence
as they howl together over the groan of traffic
in a performance of world consuming rapture
as bombers in the art war, and they empty churches,
strip the Klan to its skin, deface
the tonal scale and the art of the line
and love the explosions scattering miles below.

U.S. Signal Corps Footage
For Hollis Frampton

The sun went down for hours on Silver Lake
through low clouds and the sun path on the water
stretched over the whole end, catching the red
and spattering it down into the small waves
the breeze made and into the wake of motor boats,
a broad slash of light that spread and spread.
My eyes changed, each light-holding ripple
became a man, a captured army rose
to the tormented surface, thousands
of prisoners when we weren't taking prisoners
on a beach in the Pacific. Our machine guns
opened on them and they fell in waves
turning the ocean red and the camera ran and ran.
I could not stop, escape. The Signal Corps
records, insists, hides and protects this film,
forced me through the bone sockets
of its theater for cleared eyes: Immerse,
it says, bring it back, absorb.

A Vision

Overnight they emptied out his street. The tall
apartment blocks are silent now: his father, mother,
his children and their daughter disappeared. Later
in a remote camp, his daughter and her husband wail
with him over the weeping child dolled up like a tart
returned for a short visit supervised by thugs.
Some special gift of insight led him to them. His driver
ditched the car and disappeared (oh you fool!)
and he darted around the streets avoiding the night patrols.

This gift, a vision of the future, erupts in one
who still conducts his life in a country without war
or revolution. Look again at the streets—flowering trees,
music bursting from windows, gleaming rows of cars,
sweet conversations humming and buzzing with peace.

The Child

I am no longer the child slashed by wire
who snaked back into the locked city
to warn Jews of the plan, the unsealing
of sealed trains, how they were killed, the camps,
the doctor-judge selecting who will die
with the flick of his white baton on the railway siding.
I screamed, Fly away! Escape! until
my throat closed, they thought me mad from loss,
everybody's loss, and brought me bread
to stop my raving—later seized by Germans
and pushed through all I had seen before, then killed.
Today I am a man in this dream
of new terror with a man's grave face,
and they believe that they must kill to live.

Ignorance

Straight black hair, olive skin,
South Asian or North African, her mouth
too composed for sensuality, with no sign
of which passion's under the composure
that she struggles for. She was so beautiful
chatter hushed when she entered.
After a swig of murky tea from a bottle
in her pack, she settled herself in her seat
on the Piccadilly line, closed her eyes
and sank in meditation on the clattering train,
her hand working away in a bag, small and gray,
she had tied to her wrist with a ribbon
and beaded string, perhaps telling beads,
perhaps setting the time for the bomb in the pack
on her lap—perhaps readying her soul
for reward in paradise. But I did not flee
the train, or that subway car, or even move
farther off. My ignorance of her mind
behind that quiet beautiful face was perfect.
I trusted that stillness and stayed still.

—London, 2006

His Balance

In the forest of towering trees
behind his high arched brow
tigers with saber teeth
and fierce brown bears
wait for a slip in his guard
to tear him apart and tear
the blood soaked liver and heart
from his warm convulsing body
his AK-47
is never far from his hands
ready even in sleep
and safe in this predator world
a jeweler with narrowed eyes
suspends with thumb and finger
a tiny brass scale
for measuring tiny things,
diamonds and flakes of gold,
flicks of the eye and of words.

Mourning Song

Lying face up to the sun
after names were collected
eyes gone to ravens
then pallid cheeks and lips
the week they lay ungathered.

The military cortege
a hundred mile progress
through the main towns,
crowds, banners, flags,
salutes with empty guns,

and the coffins at last at homes
where grief devours hearts,
the pomp stink dissipates,
descent to nowhere begins.

At The Frick

His eyes are narrowed not to miss a cue
for what to say that Henry wants to hear—
the ingratiating, serviceable face,
the richly furred language of the body
open and welcoming—Thomas Cromwell
by Holbein. Then Holbein's Thomas More
with a steady, penetrating glance, mouth
set in a skeptical turn, all wariness,
having a self to possess, possessing it.
Both men painted from life, alive
in the same room again, in New York:
More resisting the King, Cromwell saying
(no euphemisms, no disguises)
just what the King wants: Kill More.

Margaret Roper
after Holbein's drawing

To be the favorite daughter
of one like More imposes
with serene dangerous love
the curse of its obligations.
She knew her father well—
the peril of his laugh,
his last sticking point.
It made her face a dove
landing on a wire,
its white wings outspread
to drag against the wind,
her mouth the wire—
thin, wary, guarded.
She broke through the guard to More
on his last trip to the Tower
and kissed him again and again.
No one stopped her. He wrote
his last night in the Tower:
"I cumber you dear Margaret
very much....I never
liked your manner better
than when you kissed me last.
For I like when daughterly love
and dear charity
hath no leisure to look
to worldly courtesy."
Double: the gentle and ruthless
demand to protect the thing
he could no longer protect,

his head impaled on a spike
naked on London Bridge
and her last obligation—
to take it down and carry
the drained thing home
enclosed in rich cloths
and return it at last to his body.

The Killers
> *blot out their name* Deut. 9:14.

The murder of Garcia Lorca
was ordered by one man
and carried out by another
who volunteered to join
the great crusade of their people
to purify its blood
and keep their names forever
inscribed in their people's book.

Now the historians
ferret out their names
and reveal them both to the world.
It's infamy's reward.

Revile them without their names.
Obliterate both names.

The Body Politic

My husband teaches drugged, slow, violent,
and drug-slowed violent children, Special Ed,
in the race and class war of the city schools.
Through the terraced city I design
Terrace gardens high above the ground,
and yards--design, install, maintain.
A neighbor is a lawyer for the very poor,
another a broker, another a supervisor
of police, a specialist against disorder.
One makes furniture, another books,
another an old puppeteer, waves
his fingers when he speaks,
and we come together on our street to care
for our children who play with one another
in our safe circle. With a pit bull
on a tight leash one staring neighbor
in a tank top and muscled like an ex-con
with arrows, spears and guns tattooed
from his shoulders down, his whole body
military kitsch, swaggers among us
as if he were our elected protector and leader.

The Simple Life In Strongsville, Ohio
for Ralph and Louise Liske

His target was a tank column creeping
through a forest road where he'd been driven back
and he sent his men, each with a can of gas
and a flaming zippo lighter to climb a tank
pull open the hatch, dump the gas
and fling in the lighter and in every case
get himself shot. He said with brittle irony,
"One man for each tank is not bad,"
and his men return to visit every night.

We were moving to California to create
with a group of friends the 60's idea of a school
replacing need with desire, law with love,
and they sent us off with breakfast for the road,
eggs from their chickens, hand-ground coffee,
and we harvested their berries for the pancakes.
The simple life in the Quaker manner braced
his fragile grip on an ordered life. His wife
explained, his men return to visit every night.

Reading Faust When Young
for David Mamet

I remember only the leap from the bridge
into the turbulent river after knowledge,
but not what special knowledge or what power
ever came his way in the old story.
I was young when I read it. Immortality
meant art and Faustus was never an artist.
And as for girls, you didn't need the devil,
when you offered everything. What did he really
need to know? Something about the girl—
what she felt and could never say because
she had no words for it? He had little
to say to the Greats. Helen was a peep-show.
And the stuff about his soul—
well, that was religious and historical.

Overreaching for me was natural. I wanted
to know everything, to stay forever in school
taking courses. God and the devil
never figured in. With his snaky tail
the devil was too fanciful to explain
the lines waiting for gas or a bullet and ditch
and fire bombs and carpet bombs and the icy
rapture of ideologues shouting about who to kill
and who to save. My fellow humans were real:
their evil was sufficient. The sacred
was love and art and the political dream.
The world-drunk heart was what I took for the soul,
which dulled the edge of Faustus' sacrifice
and god was never real enough to love or lose.

After The Revolution

They both held a silence at separate windows
breathing so softly that the faint
rush of air would not interfere
with the fluting of the thrushes back and forth
across the four corners of the garden,
and savored together the *lente, lente,*
the darkening room, the bird song
in the middle distance and the crescent moon
rising. Their silence in this vigil was important.
His voice had grown mechanical
and oppressed him with his own spirit's death
laboring for a cause that changed and changed.
He was once so passionate in battle
and beautiful, Trotsky said his eyes alone
were revolution in the name of more perfect love.
That was the evening he disappeared.
She never knew when he left the room,
whether the Security Police arrived
and he went out to meet them, or merely walked
into something unofficial,
a new life or death in the newest order,
the moon behind a cloud, nothing and silence.

Child Soldiers

The old ones, the artists who hobble, poets, composers
who believe in the well tempered scale, the visible world
of angels and virgins, women who dress to reveal the State,
faces that display a self, the self, and language
with measured music bodying visions of measure,
all dragged from their homes and crammed in boxes
called "little ease" in which one cannot sit or lie
and lined up for public ridicule
while the young screw the old muses in new positions
and make arrangements to dispose of the hard cases —
use even younger artists, children:
I began to sing to them when they entered
with their automatic rifles, small but efficient,
but the children who had been told to kill me killed me.

WAR WORK (Brooklyn, 1945)

I woke one night, after Hiroshima,
to a great noise and saw the sky turn white
then red. I ran to my parents room,
they were awake and talking in their bed
and yelled that they had dropped an atom bomb
on Manhattan. From my war work
even at eight years old I knew the right direction.
Father and I were masters of the deck
of aircraft silhouettes for rooftop spotters.
We quizzed each other, learning to distinguish
the slender Messerschmitt from Mustang,
all the Stukas, Heinkels, Junkers,
the chunky Flying Fortress and the long
Dornier bombers and we all loved
our Lockheed Lightning with its twin booms.

From the roof of our apartment house we saw
only the Parachute Jump in Coney Island
and the sun-struck Empire State and Chrysler towers.
If we saw German planes (we never did)
we could calculate their air speed
and figure out their payload.

I kept a cool head as I shook in fear.
They said it was a storm, thunder, lightning,
and led me back to bed but I knew my parents
lied to pacify me. I stayed awake,
beyond comfort in the oncoming dawn,
and heard the fearful murmur of their talk.

The Information Age
"Trust us." the NSA

About you we know a great deal
said Intelligence behind its desk,
knowing what I don't know. I writhed.

A careless stance is eloquence:
I saw my profile leap,
wrinkled shirt, cargo pants,
from an instant metadata sweep.

The official face across the desk
is a dataset as legible
as shuffle, stoop, swagger, stride;
an algorithm coded in my city
childhood lets me read this dog.

To read or be read,
inform or misinform, a grin,
an ice face, cover and uncover,
a kiss on the smartphone,
dance, are data you can't hide.

As in the Old Time, when
she knew once she saw my face,
the smile, helpless stare, stopped
breath, that I knew she was dying.
It's how she learned she was dying.

Diplomacy

Their smiles are coded: *of course, surely, never,*
one *but.* Their stern attention a bored charade:
they know what will be said and what each player
must say back and what face must be played.
It takes a life in a leisured, pampered class
to master this savage skill, so superior to war.

April 26, 2006

This is the day I reach 69,
the elegant union of head to tail, tail to head,
the lover's number, the yin-yang sign,
a celebration of three, the mystic number
of the guide through the forbidden grove (now allowed)
to the freely disregarded former god
who was absent from any supervisory role
in the century in which I've lived most of my years
on an orderly, ritual-loving continent,
with well regulated trash collection,
public gardens, smooth lawns, milk
delivered at dawn in cold bottles, clinking and sweating—

screaming and glistening with blood
at the hour of my birth Guernica was carpet bombed
as practice for the time of saturation—
the horrified face through the window that sees
the broken bodies by the light of a bare bulb—
devastating cities thick with targets, human
and other items of civil life: school,
public sculpture in parks, music pavilion, musician,
library, literary life, the writer.

The Entitled
> *Lord John Stuart and his Brother, Lord Bernard Stuart*
> painted by van Dyck

Two boys, fair curled hair, brash eyes,
jewels and gold embroidered clothes (the lace
alone would feed all the poor of London)
are a vision of self-pleasure and assurance.
Their necks are long and slender, their arms thin,
their fingers crusted with rings and long.
It is not their strength we see but comfort
with their weakness. They will ruin
everything they touch and fail without pain.

Heritage *for Kaliane*

She is named for the destroyer, Kali,
who wears the cost of love and beauty,
a scarf of severed heads with hands
dangling from her belt, drunk on the blood
of a head she holds aloft and pours into her mouth,
her curved sword shines through gouts of blood,
Kali, whose sacred place, the crematorium,
flaunts our violence.

Her father's father, in his nineties, sits
near her at a table among a crowd
of languages and capable in all of them.
He escaped the Nazi death camps
(bloodless, the cutting off of breath)
eluded the French with his Hungarian name—
the Milice never dreamed he was a Jew—
and raised his family in the maze of Paris.

Her mother's parents fled to Paris before
murder was decreed by Pol Pot
for those whom education made unfit
for the clean slate he needed to invent the State:
the photographs recording who must die,
the tied hands, the bullet to the brain
or suffocation in a plastic bag.
(bloodless, the cutting off of breath).

Half Cambodian, half Hungarian Jew,
she laughs aloud at the confusion
that she partly feels, knowing what she knows

about the past, yet her present shines
with promise—lovely Parisian, multilingual,
new Sorbonne degree.
My existence (laugh) *is so improbable.*
I don't know how I'm here. Or why.

The Marrano

> *Art is a remedy for the worst diseases of the mind,*
> *the corruption of consciousness.*   R.G. Collingwood

God wants the souls of the faithful,
not their corpses. He has carrion enough.
In *The Golem* it explains
from moments of the highest danger
he saves us, always in the form of wonders,
like making a new man.   For this truth
we struggle in disguise.
I moved to Hamburg or Seville, bought
a bakery or clothing store, a new name,
and lived openly, spoke like a native. I was
a kind of native, the most internal exile.
I could not change my name
because I was committed to disguise,
from Weiss to Scheiss, Hermano to Marrano.
I am his pig. To hide Him I renounce Him.
My teacher cared for me, a prize student.
To spare my feeling he asked me to leave the class
during his diatribes against the Jews.
I listened from the hallway, grateful
for this lesson in accommodation.
Modesty and secrecy are virtues of the chosen.
Study the pig for modesty. The cat
buries the emblem of the world. We learn
in secret through closed doors, all love.
I welcome the need to convert, create
an adequate corruption of the mind
fit for understanding, for the sacred,
the one text, the one ungainly text,

saying *Alles in ordnung ist,*
meaning another, unimaginable order.
The Gnostics were right, the world is made of shit.
I made my life a work of art expressing this.

From The Book Of Blessings

Hear, O Israel, the divine abounds
everywhere and dwells
in everything: the many are one.
The blind giant swells

proceed across the dispassionate ocean
and scour shores of tree
and house, of humans and their works—
without conscience or memory—

with divine indifference. Rampant cells
in lung and brain and breast
are fruitful and multiply the same divine
unconcern for their withering host.

The divine abounds in the press of bodies
where touch increases terror—
driven with clubs into a dark room—
divine—the tight door

that seals behind them—their prayer
whose echo tumbles and roars
in the cement room—divine the gas—
divine the man who pours.

The Execution Of Lady Jane Grey (after a painting by Paul Delaroche, 1795-1856)

When my draft board inquired if any
mental condition made me unfit for the army,
in ignorance I wrote that I could never
give or accept a stupid or cruel order.
With no war near they didn't bother with me:
innocent, hopeful, visionary, blind.
I still fail to grasp violence with my mind,
incapable of the politics of any possible world.

Under a blindfold the girl is drugged by panic
as her hands grope for where she must lay her neck.
One waiting woman hides her face against the wall.
Another faints. The headsman looks on, professional,
concerned to make a clean job for a queen,
and the priest reassures her about her sudden return
to God as he guides her hand to the block. Everyone
is beautifully dressed. The stage lights are on Jane.

This is the decorative face of violence.
How deeply pathos suffuses the scene. No
blood yet, no wall of flaming jet fuel racing across a room
driving you out the ninetieth floor window.
No roll call to witness a hanging, on your forearm
no numbers. I thought at first: how did they find two
empty planes? I could not imagine passengers.

Ancient City

The tough testicular fruit and broad leaves
of strangler figs and smothering vines cancel
all light, and poisonous moss eats
the delicious flesh of stone bodies that fill
temple walls with attitudes of sexual ecstasy
    (disciplined abandon
        in their balance, faces
            in contemplation of their pleasure)
and here I first learned to incarnate
those stone women in my arms or climbing
up my trunk to form the great sexual tree.

And from their dreaming faces--
among them one face with an open-mouthed smile
    (and all the while
        I applied my studies
            to warm bodies)
in that face, and in the faces in my hands, with my whole
body I entered the struggle for true feeling
    (and all the while
        I strolled in the broad streets
            losing myself in music, rapt by theater)
among the ornate walls built my own inner life, set out
its real boundaries, within the civic space,
the porch, cafe, temple, the temple wall,
the need to understand the masquerade of faces,
to fight careless or willful decomposition of words.

My city, after a few human lifetimes was reabsorbed
by the wildness it walled out, remains as words.

Scandal

The opposition party, conservative and upright,
whose organs of increase run their lives the same
way ours do, lie about it more ingeniously.
They impeach us with the same shameful delights
we all share, their embarrassments and pleasures.
Our philosophers with their love of truth assert
the necessity, logical and empirical, of lying
before, during, after copulation
and leave us helpless with our innocent candor.
Our opponents stay silent, decorous,
as though our world's body spreads open
to their wishes without a thought of its own.

Gesualdo In Concert

In a Protestant Church in Paris, bare walls,
large wooden Cross without Christ,
a lectern for pulpit, ornate the Gesualdo
erotic and liturgical madrigals
reverb off these walls in his unique
archaic and invented modes, so outlandish
no composer dared to use them again
for three hundred years. They weren't singing
just the vowels. With him one sings
the whole passionate word. He is the exemplary Catholic
for his Protestant hosts: intricate
mind, highly wrought ecstatic music,
a multiple murderer (his wife, her lover,
Duke of Andria, and suspected others),
a sadist and devoted masochist,
a compact of depravity. Audience agog,
a girl at my side hardly breathing
to create a silence that makes way for the music
and she is staring with her whole face,
eyes and mouth agape, nostrils flaring,
to see, to taste, to smell the music,
and here, histories of bloody enmity—
Catholic and Protestant, Hindu,
Moslem, Jew, are transfixed by discordant
harmonies and stunned to a fleeting truce.

Burmese Temple Bell

Each dawn this great bell
is struck for each sin
one hundred eight blows:
the world is gathered in
the circle of its voice
and everywhere within
a great order rung.
It tolls through the school
where sleepy children learn
the ciphers and the rule
to wear inside the face,
not rule but sub-rule
that they can never break.
They chant in unison,
breathe in its metal breath,
their cheeks to its brass skin.
My own careless life,
summoned by this bell
with its low resonance,
from dreaming half awake
or dawdling with words in a room,
would lose the small self,
the small waste of time
in that trembling embrace and dance
that calls me whole to home.

Meditations on Violence

Meditations On Violence

Too near the ancient troughs of blood
Innocence is no earthly weapon.
                              Geoffrey Hill

   Thou hast beat me out
Twelve several times, and I have nightly since
Dreamt of encounters twixt thyself and me--
We have been down together in my sleep
Unbuckling helms, twisting each others throat--
And wak't half dead with nothing.
                    Aufidius in *Coriolanus*

1

THE HISTORY OF DOVES IN OUR TIME

The doves batter themselves against the big wind
but make no headway toward their nests in the eaves
and they circle and plunge and are driven back
above the roof like children trying to force
their bodies through a close police line
who are hurled back at every lunge and feint
and scramble up screaming and try again before
they scatter in terror as their parents cry out their names
from the other side of the line. The big storm
is racing across the wide plains where no trees
or hills slow its force, its wall of wind. It will be
an even worse time to be helpless and far from home.

2

"Being young," he said, dreading himself,
"persuaded it was right, too young
to tell, myself, if it *was* right,
I could do it knowing I had to do it--
I've known in football deadly competitive rage,
knowing the other team was vermin,
their lives or ours, and this knowledge
enabled me, enabled me to do and do...

"I've seen my uncles cry
over what they did in Vietnam--
burning men in holes, exploding bodies,
when they were too young to tell,
as friends burned and burst around them.
And if I had to do it I could do it."

Then a capricious turn against his dread--
bravado, a strained smile, a cocked head.

3

THE HEALING ART
   comical-tragical-epical-historical

When Prince Andrei dies, millions mourn,
each in his chair, alone, the great weight
of *War and Peace* resting in their hands,
reading of his wounds and fever
and the cruel tease--full life, young son,
great heart reopened after grief,
wrenched from him, and how severe
and inevitable his death appears--
though with his skeptical turn,
skill at handling intricate affairs,
he could have held back from battle.

Chekhov was enraged at Andrei's death.
He knew the modern way to drain infection,
that this death was medically unnecessary,
he, himself, could have saved his man.
Only a cruel art would contrive
(Oh, Tolstoi!) to kill Andrei.
He could have blinded him and let him live.

4

This handsome boy will die
because he must avenge
himself his father's murder
in a village near Durango.
Now he is here to study
in Palo Alto High
loved in the Quaker home
that shelters him from his past
by the frightened daughter who sees
in his silence his assent
to the unbetrayable task
and tastes the hate in his kiss.
His gifts will lead him on
swiftly through medical school--
not haunted but possessed
by the clear pastoral code
and the cool, simple skill
that rushes the dead man's son
to kill his father's killer
and tumble ahead in the race.
As he shoots the man at his table
he will make the same choice
his father's killer did
and leave the son alive
who, when he's fully prepared,
will kill him in his clinic
in a village near Durango
as he lances a child's boil
that splashes over his coat
while he looks up with annoyance
and dies with the same surprise.

5

LETTER FROM WITWATERSRAND
    From a friend after the massacre at Sharpeville:

"The exit wounds were all in front. They issued
an order that stood me and a rifle
on guard from midnight to dawn over our
suddenly less venerable school.
If this rifle is stolen my sentence
is seven mandatory years. With my
wife and two children in the house
there's no doubt in which direction I
am forced to shoot. Understand, today
I'm damned. The wounds were all enormous.
Breasts and whole faces blown away."

Signed: *"Pudendum Africanus."*

6

SMALL WARS
    "Thank God for Numbers." Jane Austen on war news.

Dozens of deaths, only,
or a few hundred or thousand
we now call low-intensity conflict:

we can obtain the totals—snipers
against tanks, bystanders,
skeletal children in torched villages.

To count is to grasp, to enable
the shattered body to enter
a stiffened mind. A solvent of sorts.

What we call great
or total war, is when we lose
count—several millions,

several, several millions
screaming, half on fire, crushed in rubble,
become innumerable and disappear.

7

At The Memorial

I looked for one name, a former student
from the early 'adviser' years of the war
who derailed himself to Vietnam
in an aimless time, looking for something more
than a pallid student life at a seminar table.
I heard he died from one who heard he died,
so in faint columns etched in the dark wall
I searched for a name attached to a clever boy
and with slow repeated blows inside my skull
all those names attached themselves to people
as the numerousness gathered its human weight
joking and leaning on the table.

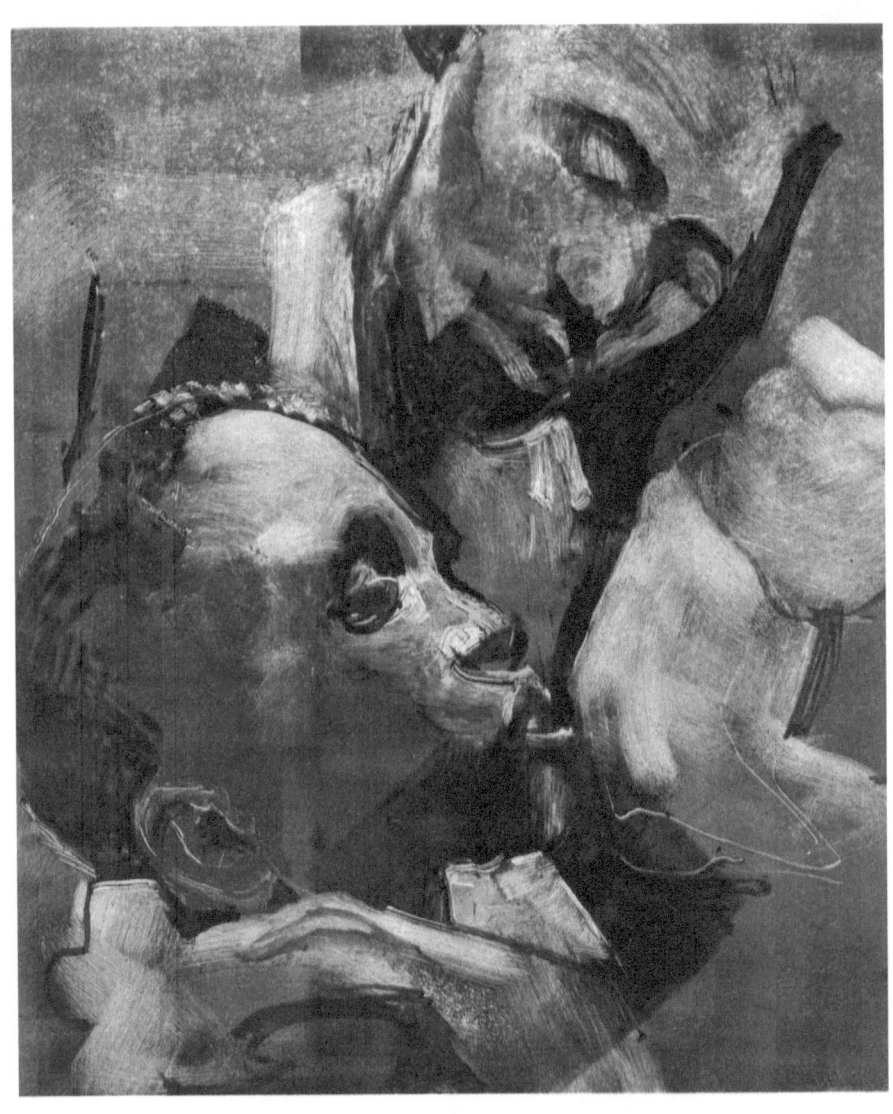

8

MACHINE GUN NEST
>In 1962, when this encounter took place, Paul Smith
>had recently retired from the *San Francisco Chronicle*.
>Under his editorship it had won 17 Pulitzer Prizes.

Every man was dead over his gun in this nest.
Eisenhower hauled the press corps there
to purge their cruel wit and urge them to awe
at this supreme devotion, said Paul Smith,
who was hauled there and awed.
He wanted to awe his high-minded guests
and their pretty students at his house on Partington Ridge
above Big Sur overlooking the violent Pacific.
(I was enchanted by its wilderness and elegance,
the rattlesnake disposed of on the patio with a shotgun,
the circle of tall, beautiful women in long
black handwoven dresses and gold cigarettes,
chic, bored.)
                    But we were Pacifists,
anti-tests-anti-war-anti-bomb
against "advisers" in Vietnam. Antic and active.
I could not get past my outrage
that no one could see clearly the this and that
to prevent the World War. Those men
should not have been there, draped on their guns
clogging them with blood. It was simple.
That simple. I denied their heroism.
Smith pounded on the table to make me see.

The students wandered away. Adults in battle
like parents' fights, were frightening,
and their lives also hung in this balance,
so I too shouted and would not see.

9

Before it fell I moved through the burnt halls
and large desolate rooms among the shells
of desks and steel beams where walls were
and in the eye-throat-and-lung-singeing smells,
first walking, then running till I was breathless,
desperate for something alive in this shell of a tower,
ash floors, beams and all metal still glowing red,
and clothes, flesh and small bones burnt off the dead.

10

les enfants aussi, the children too: a notation in pencil
by Pierre Laval on the order for deportation of Jews from
Vichy France to Auschwitz

Plodding, with heavy luggage, in dark suits
before their patient wives, who, unruffled,
with broad Brooklyn accents, keep order
among their many children with orderly curls;
the older ones, decorous, mannerly,
thoughtful, subdued, *les enfants aussi*.

The fathers fold away their dark coats,
and bury themselves in men's work, study
and prayer. Our flight to London is crammed
with Orthodox American Jews and airline security
clamps down with rigor, figuring them
a doubly delicious target—*les enfants aussi*.

I am grateful for the long delay and the rumble
below in the baggage hold, and the explosive
sniffing dogs, better friends to man
than man. There are no innocent Americans, say
the scourge of infidels, who're free
with God's vengeance: *les enfants aussi*.

11

Photo Exhibit in Soho, Nov. 2001

There are few corpses here. What we are shown
is mourners and rescuers and the crime against real estate,
the firemen's priest killed performing the rites
over a fireman killed by a leaper, and then the leapers.
Mostly it's the massed communal grief
that multiplies the solitude of grief, faces
sobbing or seeking or stopped in unbelief.
Bloody survivors. The dead are what we breathe.

12

The Massacre

The journalists lied about the numbers.
They said hundreds were killed,
unarmed, facing the world
with the force of their souls, and the wall
of guns, against all rules, opened fire.
Historians say that only 44 were killed.
Ramon was among them and he alone was 97 dead,
Roberto at a low estimate was 86,
and Arturo the precious whom everyone loved,
six of whose odes will last forever,
there is no counting the number of deaths of Arturo.

About the Author

Barry Goldensohn is the author of eight collections of poems. He has taught at Goddard College, Iowa Writers' Workshop, Hampshire College and Skidmore College. When not at home in Cabot, Vermont, he can be found in Berkeley, NYC, Paris or London with his wife, the poet and scholar, Lorrie Goldensohn.

About the Artist

Douglas Kinsey is a painter and monotyper. He has exhibited throughout this country as well as in England, Sweden and Japan. His illustrations have mostly been for books of poetry. For twelve years he has been a Professor Emeritus at the University of Notre Dame, but early on he taught in the University of North Dakota as well as in the colleges of Berea and Oberlin. He is also a musician who plays early music.

Fomite

A fomite is a medium capable of transmitting infectious organisms from one individual to another.

"The activity of art is based on the capacity of people to be infected by the feelings of others." Tolstoy, What Is Art?

Writing a review on Amazon, Good Reads, Shelfari, Library Thing or other social media sites for readers will help the progress of independent publishing. To submit a review, go to the book page on any of the sites and follow the links for reviews. Books from independent presses rely on reader to reader communications.

For more information or to order any of our books, visit
http://www.fomitepress.com/FOMITE/Our_Books.html

More Books from Fomite...

Joshua Amses — *Raven or Crow*
Joshua Amses — *The Moment Before an Injury*
Jaysinh Birjepatel — *The Good Muslim of Jackson Heights*
Jaysinh Birjepatel — *Nothing Beside Remains*
Antonello Borra — *Alfabestiario*
Antonello Borra — *AlphaBetaBestiaro*
Jay Boyer — *Flight*
Mike Breiner— *The Way None of This Happened*
David Brizer — *Victor Rand*
Paula Closson Buck — *Summer on the Cold War Planet*
David Cavanagh — *Cycling in Plato's Cave*
Dan Chodorkoff — *Loisada*
Michael Cocchiarale — *Still Time*
James Connolly — *Picking Up the Bodies*
Greg Delanty — *Loosestrife*
Catherine Zobal Dent — *Unfinished Stories of Girls*
Mason Drukman — *Drawing on Life*
J. C. Ellefson — *Foreign Tales of Exemplum and Woe*
Tina Escaja — *Free Fall/Caida Libre*
Marc Estrin — *Speckled Vanities*

Fomite

Zdravka Evtimova — *Carts and Other Stories*
Zdravka Evtimova — *Sinfonia Bulgarica*
Anna Faktorovich — *Improvisational Arguments*
John Michael Flynn — *Off to the Next Wherever*
Derek Furr — *Suite for Three Voices*
Derek Furr — *Semitones*
Stephen Goldberg — *Screwed and Other Plays*
Barry Goldensohn — *The Hundred Yard Dash Man*
Barry Goldensohn — *The Listener Aspires to the Condition of Music*
R. L. Green When — *You Remember Deir Yassin*
Greg Guma — *Dons of Time*
Andrei Guriuanu — *Body of Work*
Ron Jacobs — *All the Sinners Saints*
Ron Jacobs — *Short Order Frame Up*
Ron Jacobs — *The Co-conspirator's Tale*
Zeke Jarvis — *In A Family Way*
Scott Archer Jones — *A Rising Tide of Peopl Swept Away*
Maggie Kast — *A Free, Unsullied Land*
Darrell Kastin — *Shadowboxing With Bukowski*
Coleen Kearon — *Feminist on Fire*
Jan English Leary — *Thicker Than Blood*
Roger Lebovitz — *A Guide to the Western Slope and the Outlying Areas*
Diane Lefer — *Confessions of a Carnivore*
Kate MaGill — *Roadworthy Creature, Roadworthy Craft*
Tony Magistrale — *Entanglements*
Michele Markarian — *Unborn Children of America*
Gary Miller — *Museum of the Americas*
Ilan Mochari — *Zinsky the Obscure*
Jennifer Anne Moses — *Visiting Hours*
Sherry Olson — *Four-Way Stop*
Martin Ott — *Interrogations*
Andy Potok — *My Father's Keeper*
Janice Miller Potter — *Meanwell*
Jack Pulaski — *Love's Labours*
Charles Rafferty — *Saturday Night at Magellan's*
Joseph D. Reich — *Connecting the Dots to Shangrila*

Fomite

Joseph D. Reich — *The Hole That Runs Through Utopia*
Joseph D. Reich — *The Housing Market*
Joseph D. Reich — *The Derivation of Cowboys and Indians*
Kathryn Roberts — *Companion Plants*
Robert Rosenberg — *Isles of the Blind*
Ron Savage — *What We Do For Love*
David Schein — *My Murder and Other Local News*
Peter Schumann — *Planet Kasper, Volumes One and Two*
Peter Schumann — *Bread & Sentences*
Peter Schumann — *Faust 3*
Fred Skolnik — *Rafi's World*
Lynn Sloan — *Principles of Navigation*
L.E. Smith — *The Consequence of Gesture*
L.E. Smith — *Views Cost Extra*
L.E. Smith — *Travers' Inferno*
Robert Sommer — *A Great Fullness*
Scott T. Starbuck — *Industrial Oz*
Susan Thomas — *Among Angelic Orders*
Susan Thomas — *The Empty Notebook Interrogates Itself*
Tom Walker — *A Day in the Life*
Tom Walker — *Signed Confessions*
Sharon Webster — *Everyone Lives Here*
Susan V. Weiss — *My God, What Have We Done?*
Tony Whedon — *The Tres Riches Heures*
Tony Whedon — *The Falkland Quartet*
Peter M. Wheelwright — *As It Is On Earth*
Suzie Wizowaty — *The Return of Jason Green*
Silas Dent Zobal — *The Inconvenience of the Wings*

www.ingramcontent.com/pod-product-compliance
Lightning Source LLC
Chambersburg PA
CBHW021155080526
44588CB00008B/350